Numbers 1-12

How many bunnies?

I • one

How many bunnies are **stretching**?   1   2   3

Trace **1**. Print **1**.

...ne. Print **one**.

Draw a line from **1** to each group of **1** thing.

2 : two

How many bunnies are **getting ready**?   1   2   3

Trace **2**. Print **2**.

2

Trace **two**. Print **two**.

two

Find and circle 2:

beds   books   chairs   balls

3

three

How many bunnies are **playing**?   I   2   3

Trace **3**. Print **3**.

3

Trace **three**. Print **three**.

three

Follow the path of **3s** to help the bunny get to his friends.

4

four

How many bunnies are **drawing**?   3 4 5

Trace **4**. Print **4**.

4

Trace **four**. Print **four**.

four

Draw a line to match each **number** with the correct group.

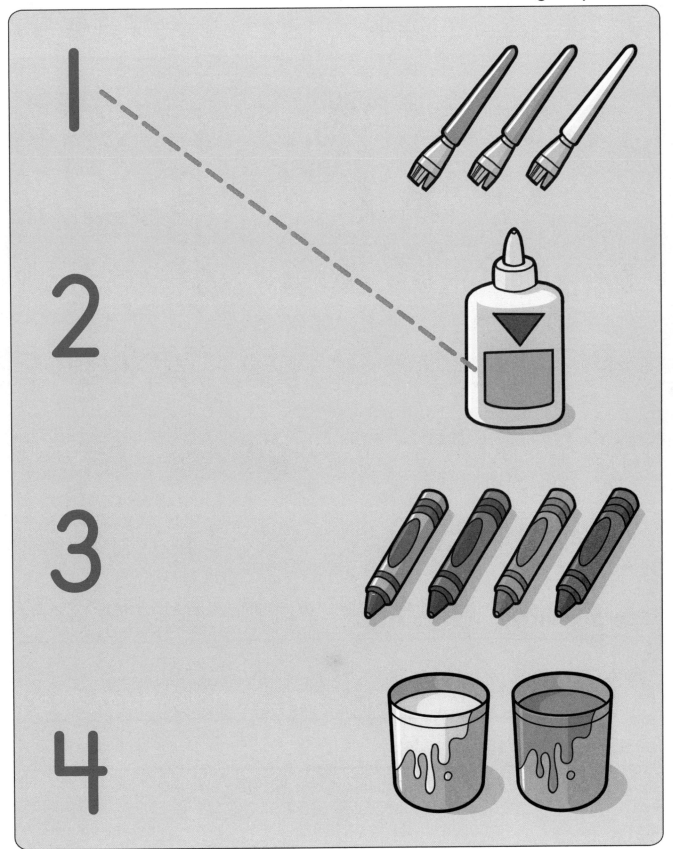

1

2

3

4

5 ●●●
●● five

How many bunnies are **on the playground**? 4 5 6

Trace **5**. Print **5**.

5 — — — — — — — — — — — — — — — — — —

Trace **five**. Print **five**.

five — — — — — — — — — — — — — — — —

Circle the groups that have **5** things.

11

6 ••• six

How many bunnies are **drinking**? 4 5 6

Trace **6**. Print **6**.

6

Trace **six**. Print **six**.

six

Use the **code** to **color** the picture.

| **1** red | **2** blue | **3** green | **4** yellow | **5** brown | **6** orange |

7

seven

How many bunnies are **playing hide-and-seek**?   7   8   9

Trace **7**. Print **7**.

7

Trace **seven**. Print **seven**.

seven

Draw a line from **7** to each group of **7** things.

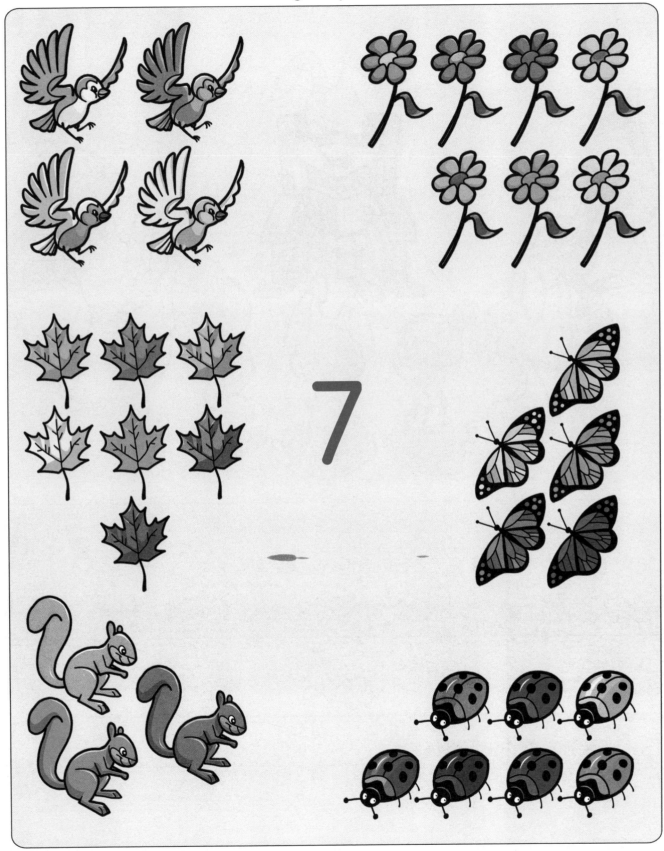

15

8

eight

How many bunnies are **listening** to the story?   7   8   9

Trace **8**. Print **8**.

8

Trace **eight**. Print **eight**.

eight

Color the Cowboy Bunny.

9

nine

How many bunnies are **napping** in the sun?   7   8   9

Trace **9**. Print **9**.

9 -

Trace **nine**. Print **nine**.

nine

Connect the dots to finish the picture. Color the toy bunny.

Can you find
and circle
the toy bunny
on page 18?

10

●●●●●
●●●●●

ten

How many bunnies are **eating snacks**?

10 11 12

Trace **10**. Print **10**.

10 -

Trace **ten**. Print **ten**.

ten -

Draw a line to match each **number** with the correct group.

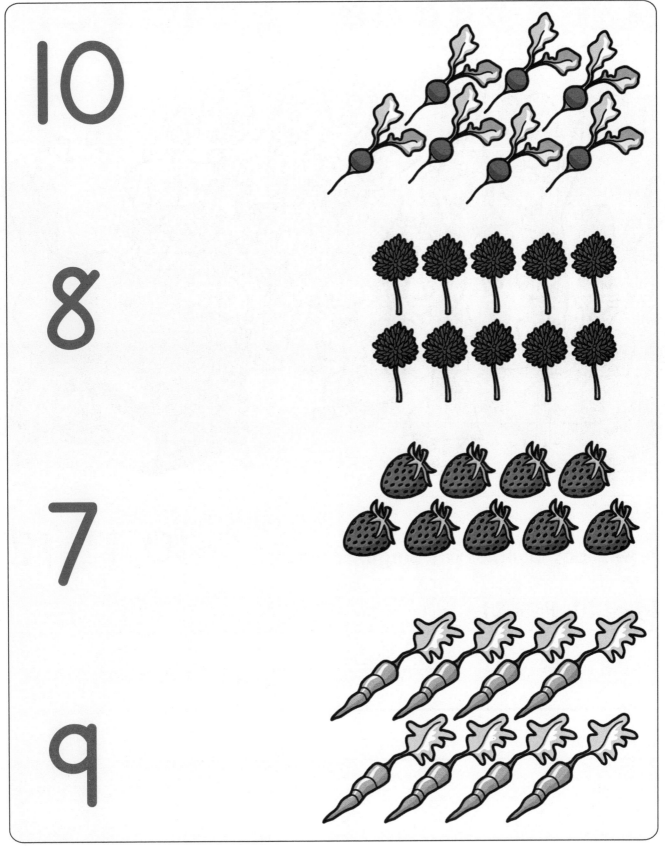

10

8

7

q

11 ••••••••••• eleven

How many bunnies are **singing**?

10 11 12

Trace **11**. Print **11**.

Trace **eleven**. Print **eleven**.

eleven

Connect the dots from 1 to 11.

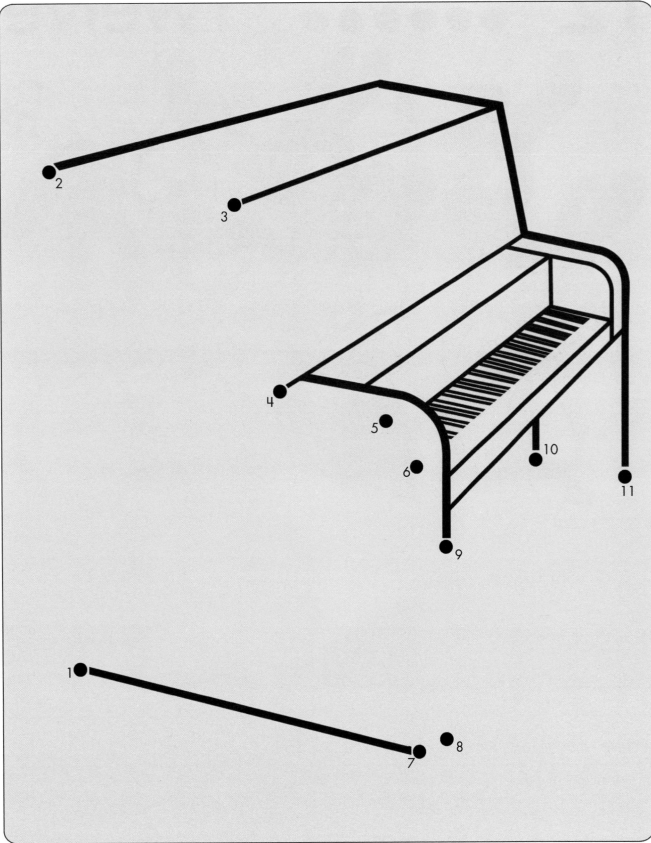

12 twelve

How many bunnies are **playing instruments**? 10 11 12

How many bunnies are **playing a flute**? 5 6 7

Trace **12**. Print **12**.

12

How many bunnies are **playing a triangle**?   1   2   3

How many bunnies are **playing a drum**?   2   3   4

Trace **twelve**. Print **twelve**.

twelve

How many bunnies are **dancing**?   10 11 12

How many bunnies have **buttons**?   1   2   3

How many bunnies are **wearing a bow tie**?   1   2   3

How many bunnies are **wearing red pants**?
1 2 3

How many bunnies are **pink**?
2 3 4

How many bunnies are **wearing a dress**?
3 4 5

How many bunnies are **at the party**?   10 11 12

How many bunnies have a **cookie**?   1 2 3

How many bunnies have a **cup**?   4 5 6

How many bunnies have a **cupcake**?

1 2 3

How many bunnies have a **hot dog**?

2 3 4

How many bunnies are **holding a balloon**?

5 6 7

Read the **words** one through six.
Circle the **number** that matches the **number word**.

one	8	3	1	0
two	9	2	6	7
three	5	4	2	3
four	7	3	5	4
five	3	5	2	1
six	6	0	3	5

Read the **words** seven through twelve.
Circle the **number** that matches the **number word**.

seven	7	12	11	5
eight	4	1	8	0
nine	2	7	6	9
ten	8	12	10	2
eleven	11	10	9	12
twelve	3	12	11	7

Family Fun Activities

These activities will provide review of the concepts
explored on the workbook pages.

1. **Counting Practice**
   As you go about daily activities with your child, look for opportunities to count things. As you stand in line at the grocery store, count the number of eggs in the egg carton, the number of apples in the bag, and the number of people waiting to check out.

2. **Make a Counting Book**
   Staple together 12 pages of blank paper. Encourage your child to write a number on each page. Ask the child to name each number and draw a corresponding number of objects on the page. Do not expect the child to complete the number pages in order or in one sitting. Instead, consider this a long-term project and add a number page each time your child becomes familiar with the number and the amount of objects associated with that number. To review the numbers, ask your child to share the book with others.

3. **Concentration**
   Using a deck of cards with the face cards removed, play a number concentration game. Begin with the numbers one through six of two suits. Explain to your child that an ace is a one. Spread the cards face down on a table. Ask the child to turn over two cards. If the cards match, the child keeps the cards and draws again. If the cards do not match, they are turned back over and play passes to the next player. When all the cards are matched, the player with the most cards wins. Add additional numbers as your child displays success at matching pairs.

4. **Number Walk**
   Help your child discover all the ways numbers are used in everyday life. Look for numbers on license plates, mailboxes, houses, mail, clocks, money, etc. Discuss how the numbers are used and what would happen if there were no numbers.

5. **Visit the Library**
   Go to your local library and help your child register for a library card. Ask the children's librarian to recommend books that reinforce numbers. Help the child find books that use numbers in the title, such as *The Three Bears* or *The Three Little Pigs*. Look for songs and poems that reinforce number concepts such as *One, Two, Buckle My Shoe* and *10 Little Monkeys Lying In Bed*.

Illustrations by
Greg Hardin

6. **Reward Stickers**
   Use reward stickers to celebrate a job well done. You or your child can choose when to place a sticker on a specific page. Use a sticker as a reward when your child completes a page that requires extra care or is a little more difficult. Your child can choose to place stickers on pages he or she is proud of completing.